Passing Through
Ellis Island

by Frank Brooks
illustrated by Matt Straub

MODERN CURRICULUM PRESS

Pearson Learning Group

Prologue

Many Americans have relatives who left their homelands in search of a new and better life in America. These people who came to America are called *immigrants*. In 1907, more immigrants came to America than ever before. During that year, more than a million people arrived in the United States.

Many of these immigrants passed through Ellis Island, which was a famous immigration center.

Many of the immigrants were poor and faced numerous tests before being allowed to remain in America. The first of these tests was the trip across the rough seas.

Once they arrived, they found themselves facing other tests. They had to prove they were healthy and were able to work hard in the United States. All of these tests were administered at Ellis Island.

Those people who passed the tests were permitted to stay and begin their new lives. Those people who did not pass were sent back to the countries they had left.

CHAPTER ONE

On ships crossing the Atlantic Ocean bound for New York, there were three classes of tickets.

Third class, or steerage, was the cheapest class. People with these tickets rode in the bottom of the ship, near the engines that made the ship go. It was hot and noisy in steerage.

Since the ship owners wanted to make a big profit, they packed as many people as they could into steerage. This section of the ship was often uncomfortable and overcrowded.

People in steerage slept in bunks, which were stacked one above the other. Food, if the people could afford it, was poor. There was very little fresh air down below, where they spent most of their time.

These were people who had never crossed the ocean before. They clung to their bunks, seasick most of the time.

Storms at sea were a hundred times scarier than any storm they had ever experienced at home. The ship pitched, or rocked, back and forth in waves that towered fifty feet above the decks. The storms lasted for days.

First-class ticket holders had rooms aboard the ships that were not much different from what they were used to at home. Many of the rooms included fancy couches, libraries of books, and finely made tables. And these people ate the best food.

People with second-class tickets slept in smaller, but private rooms. They dined in the second-class dining room where the food was good.

Those with first- and second-class tickets met immigration inspectors on board the ship. Then these passengers were quickly checked for diseases. If they were found to be healthy, they were taken straight to New York City by ferry. These people did not have to pass through Ellis Island. They almost always entered America with the Statue of Liberty welcoming them in.

To the third-class passengers, New York was still a shining city, just out of reach. One man remembers thinking that it was strange to come to a country where everyone is supposed to be equal and to find that newly arriving immigrants were not treated as equals.

The immigrants had heard so many stories about America. Some were true and some weren't.

CHAPTER TWO

During the busiest year, 1907, it was sometimes days before all the poor people were able to get off a ship. Mountains of baggage were loaded into the main building. This baggage held everything these people owned. Finding their belongings was one of the first tasks that these immigrants faced. Not everybody found the baggage they had so carefully packed. They stood in the giant brick building with only the clothes they were wearing.

Ellis Island opened its doors to greet the hopeful newcomers on January 1, 1892. Before the opening of Ellis Island, each state decided how immigrants would be accepted. During the first five years of operation, immigrants crowded into ancient wooden buildings. Then in 1897, a fire destroyed these buildings. They were rebuilt with brick and stone. They are the buildings that stand to this day.

As people entered the main building, they were asked their nationality. This question was translated into many languages. Their responses determined which line they were directed to join.

A long stairway loomed before them, twelve lines wide. They thought they were just going up to the second floor for a medical test. But in reality, the stairs were a test too.

The immigrants were watched carefully as they made their way to the second floor. There were doctors looking to see who coughed, who had to stop before reaching the top, and who limped or blinked. Doctors were watching every move!

When they reached the top of the stairs, they entered the Registry Room or Great Hall. In this room, they were lined up in long rows. The immigrants walked down narrow lanes created with rows of pipe.

As the immigrants moved along, doctors looked at them. If a person seemed healthy, the doctors looked more closely. They checked a person's legs, looking for sores. They examined a person's hands, looking for evidence of a crippling disease. They wanted to make sure that the people were healthy and that they were not bringing any diseases into this country.

While the immigrants walked through the narrow
lanes, the doctors asked and answered in their own
minds several hundred questions. If they saw any sign
of a disease, or something as minor as a crooked
finger, the fact was noted. If a problem was found,
the immigrant had to be checked by a special board
of doctors. Some had to wait days or weeks to
be cleared.

A letter written in chalk on an immigrant's clothing
was an indication that this person had a problem.
However, not *all* the problems would keep a person
out of this country. But most would.

If the doctor marked an immigrant's coat with the letter *H* it meant that the person had a heart problem. The letter *L* indicated lameness or the inability to walk properly, the letter *F* a facial rash, the letter *E* an eye disease, and the letter *X*, mental illness.

Anyone with a chalk marking was set apart from the rest of the immigrants. These people went through more medical examinations. Some of these people were sent to a hospital on Ellis Island. Once their medical problem was cleared up, they could begin their new lives in America. For others, the news was not always so good. Some people with diseases like *tuberculosis*, a lung disease, or *trachoma*, an eye disease, were sent back to their homelands. Children who were being sent back had to be taken by an adult. Deciding who would go with the child was always a hard decision.

This was a very frightening time for some people. Their dreams of beginning a new life in America were broken with the news of being returned to their homelands.

In 1907, one out of ten immigrants was returned to his or her country. Many of these people had come to this country to escape from danger. War, hunger, or hatred had been a part of their lives. Some had been sent by their families to make a new home in America. Their families were hoping to follow them soon after. Going back to the places they had left was not what they wanted.

In truth, the doctors and representatives of this country were doing what was important to protect, or guard, its citizens against terrible diseases. They wanted immigrants who could help build the country.

The people who came to Ellis Island were ready to fulfill the great promise that America represented. They had all the willpower any country could want in a new citizen. It is unfortunate that not all of them had their health.

Since most of the people arriving at Ellis Island did not speak English, translators were needed. Not knowing the language often caused frustration and confusion.

One day a mother couldn't understand why her sick child was being taken from her. She became angry and out of control. A translator was finally able to help her understand that she would see her child again.

Some translators did a better job than others did. One translator, Fiorello LaGuardia, later became mayor of New York City. He said he translated for many people, but he never got used to the sadness he saw every day.

CHAPTER THREE

As the immigrants moved along through the immigration process, they were always tense and nervous. They were afraid they would give a wrong answer to one of the inspectors or representatives and be sent back to their homelands.

After passing the medical tests, the immigrants had to stand in line for one final test, a series of questions. The immigrants had to answer questions about their occupation, their plans for earning money in the United States, the amount of money they had with them, and if anyone was meeting them.

The first question they had to respond to was, "What is your name?" Often when the immigrant's name was too difficult to say or spell, the inspector changed the name to something easier. Other times, the immigrant, who was very nervous, responded with the name of the place they came from instead of their own name. The inspector recorded what the immigrant said and, as a result, the immigrant got a new name!

After passing the final test of questions, the immigrants headed toward the money exchange. It was here that the immigrants traded their money for American money.

For the immigrants who were still part of the process, the idea of becoming an American seemed like only steps away. Although they weren't sure what was going to happen next, they were beginning to feel more confident.

Unfortunately, at this point in the process, some of the people experienced unfair treatment by those in charge. Sometimes an inspector approached an immigrant and offered to pass him or her through in return for a certain amount of money. It was usually a lot of money! Some people entered the agreement. Others could not. Offers like this confused and angered many people. At other times, the clerks behind the money exchange windows didn't always give the fair rate.

Many people came to this country to join their relatives. Often a husband would arrive first. Sometimes a whole village would raise money to send the eldest son or daughter of a family to America. In either case, the first person to arrive in America would work hard and earn enough money to bring the rest of the family across the ocean.

New arrivals on Ellis Island could send a telegraph message by cable to New York or beyond. Sometimes a relative could come to Ellis Island to "claim" the newcomer.

When people came to claim a relative, they had to bring with them papers that proved they were related. After seeing the correct papers, an inspector would ask the new immigrant a few final questions. Then the inspector would stamp the immigrant's papers and open the door. The new immigrant would pass through the wooden gate.

Even people who did not usually show affection in public often threw themselves into the arms of their relatives. This place in the main building on Ellis Island became known as "The Kissing Post."

The immigrants had passed the tests. Of course they hugged. They probably cried too!

CHAPTER FOUR

Although there were no more tests to pass, there was one more leg of the journey. The happy immigrants had to board a ferry that would take them to Manhattan. This trip was an extremely short ride, usually only about twenty minutes. It was the best part of the immigrants' journey. There was no turning back. They had made it!

Crowding on this boat ride didn't seem to bother anyone. The immigrants were very busy looking at the sights around them. They were amazed at what they saw. They had never seen such tall buildings. Excitement filled the air. These newcomers were about to start a new life. They couldn't wait!

It wasn't until the ferry docked in Manhattan, that an immigrant would dare to say, "I am in New York. I am in America."

New York was the final destination for many immigrants. But for some, it was only a stopping point before taking trains to other places.

The people who settled in New York probably settled in a part of the city where others from their homeland had settled before them. Living with people who spoke the same language, cooked the same foods, and had the same customs made the adjustment to life in a new place a little easier. The immigrants wanted a new life, but they didn't want to forget who they were!

Today, New York City is still a place where every country in the world is represented. A walk through the city can become a tour of the world. For new immigrants, neighborhoods where other immigrants from their homelands live can provide a safe starting point. From there they can learn about America among friends and family.

Four out of ten American families have a relative who passed through Ellis Island. Many of these immigrants who passed through Ellis Island didn't say much about the difficult journey that brought them to this country. In their minds, it was over. They felt lucky to live their lives in America.

Author's Note

My grandfather, Nathan, must have gone by Ellis Island. He was lucky enough to have been sent a second-class ticket for the ship. He met his wife, my grandmother, in the Hungarian part of New York City.

I have asked my father and my aunt many questions about Nathan. Why did he leave Hungary? What did he do when he got here? Are there relatives I have never met? I now know some of the answers to these very important questions.

If you have a relative who came here from another country, he or she might have passed through Ellis Island.

Your grandparents or great-grandparents may have gone to Chicago, Boston, or Atlanta. Many immigrants went to big cities because these places often had work for the immigrants. Or maybe your grandparents or great-grandparents were married in Europe, separated when they began their journey to America, and joined again on a farm in Iowa or Ohio.

Your relatives may be able to tell you about members of your family who came here from another country. We all have funny and sad family stories that are waiting to be discovered.

If you can find out the complete names of your great-grandparents, you've made a good start. Your telephone and computer may help you open this search and trace your roots in detail.

In 1907, there were no jets to carry people around the world. But even back then, Americans were connected to the world by a web of immigrants.

Your family is part of that web.

Ellis Island closed its doors as an immigration center on November 29, 1954. (Now newly arriving immigrants report to U.S. Government offices in cities around the country.) The last person to become a United States citizen through Ellis Island was a seaman from Norway. He stayed in New York too long and his ship left without him.

Ellis Island is now a museum. The exhibits there tell the story of the more than seventeen million immigrants who passed through Ellis Island. Outside the museum is the American Immigrant Wall of Honor. This wall contains the names of more than a half million immigrants who left their homelands in search of a better life.